BIG DOGS RULE
Labrador Retriever
Most Popular

by Jessica Rudolph

Consultant: Marianne Foote
Director Emerita, The Labrador Retriever Club, Inc.

BEARPORT PUBLISHING

New York, New York

Credits

Cover and Title Page, © Roger de la Harpe/Gallo Images/Getty Images; TOC, © Eric Isselée/Shutterstock; 4, © Jim Stevens/Bay Area Newsgroup; 5, Courtesy of Search Dog Foundation/Matt Haines; 6, Courtesy of Search Dog Foundation/California Task Force 2; 7L, Courtesy of Search Dog Foundation/California Task Force 2; 7R, Courtesy of Search Dog Foundation/California Task Force 2 8, © North Wind Picture Archives/Alamy; 9T, Courtesy of Scottie Westfall; 9B, © Mary Evans/Country Life/IPC Media Ltd/Everett Collection; 10, Courtesy The New York Public Library; 11L, © M. Wegner/Tierfotoagentur/Alamy; 11R, © Meyer/blickwinkel/Alamy; 12T, © Herbert Kratky/Shutterstock; 12B, © Denver Bryan; 13T, © Burgess Blevins/Picade; 13B, © Lynn Stone/Animals Animals Earth Scenes; 14, © NaturePL/SuperStock; 15T, © Waldemar Dabrowski/Shutterstock; 15B, © Paul J. Richards/AFP/Getty Images; 16, © Exactostock/SuperStock; 17, © Gorilla/Shutterstock; 18, © Dave Kettering/World Picture Network; 19, © Whitney Curtis Photography; 20T, © Ardea/Jean Michel Labat/Animals Animals Earth Scenes; 20B, © NaturePL/SuperStock; 21, © Juniors Bildarchiv/Alamy; 22, © Elena Elisseeva/Shutterstock; 23, © Jeannie Harrison/Close Encounters of the Furry Kind; 24, © Erin McCracken/Courier & Press; 25T, © Erin McCracken/Courier & Press; 25B, Courtesy of Guide Dogs of America; 26T, © Jim Craigmyle/Corbis; 26B, © Ardea/Jean Michel Labat/Animals Animals Earth Scenes; 27, © IndexStock/SuperStock; 28, © Minden Pictures/SuperStock; 29T, © Eric Isselée/Shutterstock; 29B, © Cathy Wilcox/Wilcox Photography; 32, © Svetlana Valoueva/Shutterstock.

Publisher: Kenn Goin
Senior Editor: Lisa Wiseman
Creative Director: Spencer Brinker
Design: Dawn Beard Creative
Cover Design: Dawn Beard Creative and Kim Jones
Photo Researcher: Mary Fran Loftus

Library of Congress Cataloging-in-Publication Data

Rudolph, Jessica.
  Labrador retriever : most popular / by Jessica Rudolph.
    p. cm. — (Big dogs rule!)
  Includes bibliographical references and index.
  ISBN-13: 978-1-61772-300-1 (library binding)
  ISBN-10: 1-61772-300-2 (library binding)
  1. Labrador retriever—Juvenile literature. I. Title.
  SF429.L3R83 2012
  636.752'7—dc22
                    2011009372

For more information, write to Bearport Publishing Company, Inc., 45 West 21st Street, Suite 3B, New York, New York 10010. Printed in the United States of America in North Mankato, Minnesota.

070111
042711CGA

10 9 8 7 6 5 4 3 2 1

Contents

Endless Energy

Things were not going well for Pearl. In 2007, the energetic Labrador retriever was living in an **animal shelter** in California. She needed a permanent home, but nobody was interested in taking her in. She just had too much energy.

Then someone from the National Disaster Search Dog Foundation (SDF) saw Pearl at the shelter. This group trains dogs to search for people buried under **rubble** after disasters occur. The SDF was looking for dogs that had enough energy and focus to search for people for hours at a time. The SDF thought Pearl would be perfect. They decided to take her into their program and train her.

◀ Pearl's full name is Black Pearl. She's called this because her fur is shiny and black like a black pearl.

Pearl's first owner sent her to the animal shelter after she jumped the fence that surrounded her home and wandered away several times.

Pearl trained every day for months with her **handler**, Ron Horetski. She learned how to work in conditions similar to ones she might face in a disaster area. She even practiced sniffing out people hiding under piles of rubble. After months of training, Pearl had learned the skills she needed to begin working as a search-and-rescue dog.

Ron helps Pearl practice climbing a ladder.

A Hero Dog

In January 2010, the SDF sent Ron and Pearl to Haiti. A huge earthquake had hit the island, causing many buildings and homes to collapse. In Haiti, Ron and Pearl were asked to search through the rubble and debris to track down **victims** who were buried underneath.

Search-and-rescue dogs look for victims trapped under several feet of rubble. After dogs find the victims, human rescuers remove the rubble and pull the people to safety. Here, Pearl and Ron walk through a collapsed building.

It wasn't an easy job, though. Pearl had to walk over pieces of sharp metal and broken glass as she used her nose to sniff out victims. She also had to watch out for deep cracks in the ground and for falling bricks. To stay safe, Pearl ignored the noises and sights around her and concentrated on her work. This was difficult to do because there were many things going on, such as other rescuers moving rubble and shouting to one another. Pearl, however, stayed focused.

For two weeks, Pearl spent hours every day looking for people buried beneath rubble.

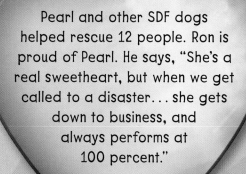

Pearl and other SDF dogs helped rescue 12 people. Ron is proud of Pearl. He says, "She's a real sweetheart, but when we get called to a disaster. . . she gets down to business, and always performs at 100 percent."

▲ **Pearl's training prepared her for walking over uneven surfaces.**

From Canada to Great Britain

It's not surprising that Pearl is such a hard worker. Her **ancestors** worked hard, too. The Labrador retriever **breed** got its start helping cod fishermen in Newfoundland, Canada, in the 1700s. At the time, the dogs were called St. John's water dogs. They were strong swimmers with short, thick **coats** that kept them warm in cold water. During fishing trips, these dogs were trained to jump into the water to catch fish that wriggled off the fishermen's hooks. They also dragged heavy fishing nets to shore.

Labrador retrievers are related to dogs that helped fishermen who fished off the Canadian island of Newfoundland hundreds of years ago.

▲ **Fishermen came from several different countries to catch codfish in the Atlantic Ocean. Icy waters and storms sometimes made the job dangerous.**

Labrador retrievers got their name in the mid-1800s. The first part of their name comes from the Labrador Sea, where the St. John's dogs used to work with fishermen. They earned the second part of their name because they like to fetch or retrieve things.

Though it's not known for sure, many people believe that British **noblemen** first noticed St. John's water dogs in the early 1800s. At that time, fishing ships carrying codfish from Newfoundland arrived in Great Britain with the St. John's dogs on board. The British were looking for better hunting dogs and learned that the dogs were good retrievers with **temperaments** and physical **characteristics** that allowed them to easily **adapt** to a hunter's needs. So they purchased some of the dogs.

In Great Britain, the St. John's dogs were **bred** to find and retrieve small **game**, such as birds and rabbits. These dogs became today's Labrador retrievers.

◀ Some historians think the St. John's water dogs may have been named after the capital city of Newfoundland—St. John's.

By the 1900s, Labradors were very poplar hunting dogs in Great Britain.

Made to Hunt and Swim

The dogs that the British noblemen bred were excellent retrievers. They had good noses for locating game and they were fast. The dogs quickly found birds that hunters shot down. They also loved to swim. If a bird that a hunter shot landed in water, a Labrador retriever could be counted on to jump in, grab the bird, and bring it back to shore in its mouth.

A Labrador helping hunters retrieve game

Labrador retrievers were first sent to the United States from Great Britain in the early 1900s. They soon became the favorite of many American hunters. Today, Labradors look very similar to the dogs that were first bred to help these hunters. They're sturdy and powerful, standing about 21.5 to 24 inches (55 to 61 cm) tall at the shoulder and weighing 55 to 80 pounds (25 to 36 kg). They also have muscular back legs that help them leap far into the water. **Webbing** between their toes, **waterproof** coats, and strong, thick tails help make them excellent swimmers.

Webbing between the toes helps a Lab push forward as it swims. ▶

◀ **Labs have powerful bodies.**

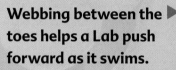

Today the **American Kennel Club** (AKC) officially recognizes the Labrador, or Lab, as part of the Sporting Group. This group includes many types of high-energy dogs that were originally bred to hunt for game in the woods and in water.

Searching for Birds

The Labradors of today continue to have strong retrieving **instincts**. Many still help bird hunters, just like their ancestors did long ago.

On land, a Labrador uses its nose to find a dead or wounded bird, such as a pheasant. Once found, the dog will retrieve the bird and bring it back to the hunter. When a Labrador finds a live bird, the dog may chase or **flush** it from its hiding place, which allows the hunter to see the bird and shoot it down.

Pheasants live in the woods and in open fields. They make their nests on the ground.

This Labrador is flushing a pheasant. Hunters teach their Labs at an early age to get used to the loud noise of a gun so they won't be afraid of the sound.

When hunting water birds, such as ducks, the hunter and the dog often hide in tall grass or in a **duck blind** near a lake. Then they wait, sometimes for hours. A well-trained Lab knows not to bark, which would frighten the birds away. When a duck finally flies overhead and the hunter shoots it, the Lab waits for the hunter's command before jumping in the water to retrieve the wounded bird.

◀ Some hunters try to attract ducks by placing floating wooden ducks called decoys in the water. Hunters, such as the one pictured, may also use a duck call. This special device sounds like a duck's quack when a person blows into it.

Labrador retrievers are bred to have "soft mouths." This means that the dog doesn't bite down on an animal or an object when carrying it in its mouth. A well-trained Labrador can even carry an egg in its mouth without breaking the shell!

13

A Special Coat

Many Labs spend their time outside in all types of weather, so it's only fitting that they have a protective coat made up of two layers. Their outercoats have hair that is short, straight, and feels hard to the touch. Their undercoats have soft hair that protects them from water, cold temperatures, and prickly shrubs in the woods. Their coats are also slightly oily and soak up very little water, keeping the dogs dry. A dry coat is lighter than a wet one, so the dogs are not weighed down and can swim more easily.

A Labrador's coat is water resistant.

The AKC recognizes only three coat colors for this breed—yellow, black, and chocolate. Yellow Labradors have fur that can be yellow, rusty red, or cream colored with darker shades of the same color on the ears, backs, and undersides. Black Labs have black fur without any other color. Chocolate Labs come in shades of light to dark brown. Although most Labs are one color, a few may have white spots on their chests or paws.

Yellow, chocolate, and black Labradors

From 1997 to 2001, a chocolate Labrador retriever named Buddy lived in the White House with President Bill Clinton and his family.

A Popular Family Dog

Although Labrador retrievers were raised to be hunters and retrievers, they also make great family pets. In fact, they have been the most popular AKC **registered** dog breed in the United States for years. Millions of Americans have Labradors as pets because they're gentle, easy to train, and like to be around people. They fit in well with families that include young children, and are even calm and friendly with strangers.

Labs love being with their families even in the snow and cold weather.

Labs also like to have lots of fun outdoors with their families. These active dogs can fetch sticks or balls for hours. They like to tag along on hiking, fishing, and camping trips, too. They especially love to play in oceans, lakes, and pools. After a long day of excitement, these lovable dogs just want to snuggle with their owners.

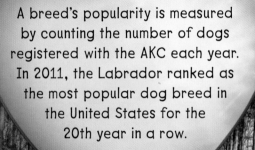

A breed's popularity is measured by counting the number of dogs registered with the AKC each year. In 2011, the Labrador ranked as the most popular dog breed in the United States for the 20th year in a row.

▼ **Labs can keep up with their owners on hiking and camping adventures.**

Splash!

Some owners enter their Labrador retrievers in competitions that highlight their dogs' love of retrieving and swimming. One competition is called **dock** diving. This event tests how far a dog can jump.

Dogs need a good running start in order to leap far into the air.

During competition, a handler stands on a dock next to a pool. He or she throws a toy in the air over the water. The dog then runs across the dock and leaps into the air after the toy. It doesn't matter if the dog catches the toy in the air or retrieves it after the toy lands in the water. What matters is the distance the dog jumps from the end of the dock to where it hits the water. Since Labs are athletic and enjoy retrieving objects, they do better than most other breeds in these competitions.

In 2010, a chocolate Lab named Jordan won a dock diving competition with a jump of 31 feet, 2 inches (9.5 m). That's almost two feet (61 cm) farther than the human long jump record!

▲ Jordan, shown here, making her winning dock dive

Labrador Litters

Adult Labs are big dogs, but they start out as tiny, helpless puppies. Females have an average of eight pups in a **litter**. The newborns' eyes are closed at first, so they can't see. In fact, they can't do much except drink milk from their mother's body. Within a couple of weeks, however, their eyes open and they begin to explore their surroundings.

▼ **Labrador mother and her litter**

Newborn Lab puppies

After four weeks, the pups have lots of energy for playing. Their retriever instincts already show at this young age, too. They can chase after balls and carry sticks in their mouths. At eight weeks old, Lab puppies are strong enough to become part of a human family.

Labradors reach their full size when they're one year old.

▲ **Labrador pups enjoy play fighting.**

Learning Good Manners

While Labradors make great pets, they need to be trained at an early age to prevent bad behavior, such as chewing on things. Young, untrained Labradors might pull on their leashes or greet people by jumping on them. A big Lab can easily knock someone down or get a person's clothes dirty.

This Lab needs to be trained to not pull on its leash.

Fortunately, Labrador retrievers are intelligent. They also like to please their owners, so it's easy to train them. For example, a Lab owner can correct a dog that likes to jump on people by saying "Off!" The owner should then gently push the dog away or turn away from it. If the dog listens, it should be rewarded with praise, treats, or belly rubs. With **consistent** training early on, Labs will quickly learn good behavior.

This Lab is being trained to sit.

Now the Lab is being trained to stay.

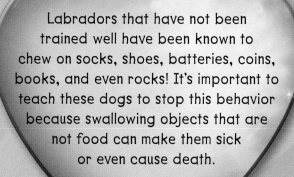

The Lab is given a treat as a reward for following directions.

Labradors that have not been trained well have been known to chew on socks, shoes, batteries, coins, books, and even rocks! It's important to teach these dogs to stop this behavior because swallowing objects that are not food can make them sick or even cause death.

Guide Dogs

Because Labs are smart and good at learning new things, many are trained to be **guide dogs**. This type of **service dog** helps **visually impaired** people get around and do things that they might not be able to do on their own. For example, a Labrador guide dog named Little Cheba helps Denise Schweizer, a teacher in Indiana. An eye disease caused Denise to lose most of her vision when she was a child. Now Denise relies on Little Cheba's help to guide her around. To do this, Denise holds on to a **harness** that's attached to Little Cheba.

Little Cheba's harness says DO NOT PET ME, I AM WORKING. Many guide dogs wear signs like this so that other people don't bother them and they can stay focused on their work. People who want to pet a guide dog should ask its owner for permission.

Denise Schweizer walks with Little Cheba down the hallway of the elementary school where she teaches.

Before Denise had Little Cheba, she tried to get around with a cane. This was especially hard to do when crossing the street. Now, however, Little Cheba can safely guide Denise across the street as well as help her do other things that she has trouble doing on her own.

◀ Denise's students love Little Cheba.

Guide dogs make it ▶ easier for visually impaired people to safely cross the street.

A Happy Family Member

Labrador retrievers are loyal, hard working, loving, and make a great addition to any family. However, these dogs are a big responsibility, too. They need lots of attention and exercise. Labradors also **shed** their coats a fair amount and need regular brushing. Trips to the **veterinarian** are necessary to keep them healthy as well.

◀ **Older Labs may have problems with their hips or knees. This is common with dogs that spend years running and jumping. Regular trips to a veterinarian help Labs stay healthy.**

Labs love to play in water. If an owner doesn't live near a lake, river, ocean, or pool, a small wading pool or even a sprinkler and hose will make a Labrador retriever very happy.

For people willing to take on these responsibilities, Labs offer big rewards. They are great playmates, willing to hunt, swim, or play fetch with their owners. They also are wonderful companions, happy to curl up next to their owners and cuddle. So for active people who want a great **canine** friend, Labrador retrievers are hard to beat.

Labrador retrievers often seem to have smiles on their faces.

Labrador Retrievers at a Glance

Weight:	55–80 pounds (25–36 kg)
Height at Shoulder:	21.5–24 inches (55–61 cm)
Coat Hair:	Short, straight, thick outercoat; soft, weather-resistant undercoat; some Labradors may have slightly wavy fur down their backs
Colors:	Black, yellow, or chocolate, sometimes with white markings on the chest or feet; yellow Labradors may have darker shades of color on their ears, backs, and undersides
Country of Origin:	Canada
Life Span:	About 12–13 years
Personality:	Outgoing, eager to please, gentle, calm, loves the company of people, playful

Best in Show

What makes a great Labrador retriever? Every owner knows that his or her dog is special. Judges in dog shows, however, look very carefully at a Labrador's appearance and behavior. Here are some of the things they look for:

eyes are kind, friendly, intelligent, and alert

nose is wide

ears are set back, hanging close to the head, not large and heavy

tail is thick at the top, thinner at the bottom; rounded in shape

head is wide with powerful jaws

neck and shoulders are muscular

thighs are powerful

outercoat is short, straight, and thick

feet are strong with webbing between the toes

Behavior: friendly, gentle, intelligent, easygoing

Glossary

adapt (uh-DAPT) to change to fit the environment

American Kennel Club (uh-MER-uh-kuhn KEN-uhl KLUHB) a national organization that is involved in many activities having to do with dogs, including collecting information about dog breeds, registering purebred dogs, and setting rules for dog shows

ancestors (AN-sess-turz) family members who lived a long time ago

animal shelter (AN-uh-muhl SHEL-tur) a place that houses homeless or lost animals

bred (BRED) when dogs from specific breeds are mated to produce young with certain characteristics

breed (BREED) a kind of dog

canine (KAY-nine) a member of the dog family

characteristics (*ka*-rik-tuh-RISS-tiks) typical qualities or features

coats (KOHTS) fur or hair on dogs or other animals

consistent (kuhn-SISS-tuhnt) behaving in the same way

dock (DOK) a landing area; usually where ships load and unload goods

duck blind (DUHK BLINDE) a small structure made of grass or brush or a hole in the ground in which hunters hide as they wait for ducks to appear

flush (FLUHSH) to cause something to take flight suddenly

game (GAME) wild animals hunted for sport or food

guide dogs (GIDE DAWGZ) dogs that have been trained to live with and accompany people who are blind or nearly blind, allowing the people to move about safely

handler (HAND-lur) a person who trains and works with animals

harness (HAR-niss) a device attached to an animal that allows people to hold on to the animal

instincts (IN-stingkts) knowledge and ways of acting that an animal is born with and doesn't have to learn

litter (LIT-ur) a group of baby animals, such as puppies, that are born to the same mother at the same time

noblemen (NOH-buhl-men) people of high rank

registered (REJ-uh-sturd) to be officially listed with an organization

rubble (RUHB-uhl) broken pieces of rock, brick, and other building materials

service dog (SUR-viss DAWG) a dog that is trained to do daily tasks for a person who has disabilities or health problems

shed (SHED) to have hair or fur fall off the body

temperaments (TEM-pur-uh-muhnts) personalities, qualities, or natures

veterinarian (*vet*-ur-uh-NER-ee-uhn) a doctor who takes care of dogs and other animals

victims (VIK-tuhmz) people who have been hurt or killed by someone or something

visually impaired (VIZH-oo-uh-lee im-PAIRD) having very weakened eyesight or being completely blind

waterproof (WAW-tur-PROOF) able to keep water from passing through

webbing (WEB-ing) skin between the toes that helps with swimming

Bibliography

Pavia, Audrey. *The Labrador Retriever Handbook*. Hauppauge, NY: Barron's Educational Series (2001).

Thomas, E. Donnall. *Hunting Labs*. Minocqua, WI: Willow Creek Press (2003).

www.akc.org/breeds/labrador_retriever/index.cfm

www.thelabradorclub.com

Read More

George, Charles and Linda. *Labrador Retriever*. New York: Scholastic (2010).

Larrew, Brekka Hervey. *Labrador Retrievers*. Mankato, MN: Capstone Press (2009).

Mathea, Heidi. *Labrador Retrievers*. Edina, MN: Checkerboard Books (2010).

Learn More Online

To learn more about Labrador retrievers, visit
www.bearportpublishing.com/BigDogsRule

Index

About the Author

Jessica Rudolph has edited many books about animals. She lives in Arizona with a Great Dane named Boris and an English setter named Sawyer.